United States Presidents

Grover Cleveland

Paul Joseph
ABDO Publishing Company

visit us at
www.abdopub.com

Published by Abdo Publishing Company, 4940 Viking Drive, Edina, Minnesota 55435.
Copyright © 2001 by Abdo Consulting Group, Inc. International copyrights reserved in all countries. No part of this book may be reproduced in any form without written permission from the publisher.

Printed in the United States.

Photo Credits: Corbis, A/P Wide World

Contributing Editors: Tamara L. Britton, Kate A. Furlong, Christine Phillips
Book design and graphics: Patrick Laurel

Library of Congress Cataloging-in-Publication Data

Joseph, Paul, 1970-
    Grover Cleveland / Paul Joseph.
        p.   cm. -- (United States presidents)
    Includes index.
    Summary: Follows the life of the minister's son who rose from being an
honest city lawyer to serve two terms as American president.
    ISBN 1-57765-249-5
    1. Cleveland, Grover, 1837-1908--Juvenile literature. 2. Presidents--United States--
Biography--Juvenile literature. [1. Cleveland, Grover, 1837-1908. 2. Presidents.] I.
Title. II. Series: United States presidents (Edina, Minn.)
E697.J67   1999
973.8'5'092--dc21
    [B]   98-21105
                                                    CIP
                                                     AC

Contents

Grover Cleveland

*G*rover Cleveland was the twenty-second and twenty-fourth president of the U.S. He is the only president to serve two terms that were not in a row.

Cleveland worked as a lawyer and a sheriff. He served as mayor of Buffalo, New York. Then he was elected New York's governor.

In 1884, Cleveland was elected president. He was the first **Democrat** to be elected in 24 years. He fought for the **gold standard**. This made him unpopular. He lost the next election.

Then Cleveland and his wife moved to New York. They started a family. Cleveland worked as a lawyer. Then the Democrats **nominated** him for president again.

In 1892, Cleveland won the election. Soon after, a **depression** began. Cleveland tried to end it. But some of his actions angered Americans. He decided not to run for a third term.

Cleveland retired in Princeton, New Jersey. He gave speeches, wrote, and spent time with his family. He died on June 24, 1908.

President Grover Cleveland

Grover Cleveland (1837-1908)
Twenty-second and Twenty-fourth President

BORN: March 18, 1837

PLACE OF BIRTH: Caldwell, New Jersey

ANCESTRY: Scots-English, Irish

FATHER: Richard Falley Cleveland (1804-1853)

MOTHER: Ann Neal Cleveland (1806-1882)

WIFE: Frances Folsom (1864-1947)

CHILDREN: Five: 2 boys, 3 girls

EDUCATION: Public schools

RELIGION: Presbyterian

OCCUPATION: Lawyer

MILITARY SERVICE: None

POLITICAL PARTY:	Democrat
OFFICES HELD:	Erie County assistant district attorney, sheriff of Erie County, mayor of Buffalo, governor of New York
AGE AT INAUGURATIONS:	47 and 55
YEARS SERVED:	1885-1889 and 1893-1897
VICE PRESIDENTS:	Thomas A. Hendricks (1885) and Adlai E. Stevenson (1893-1897)
DIED:	June 24, 1908, Princeton, New Jersey, age 71
CAUSE OF DEATH:	Heart attack

Detail Area

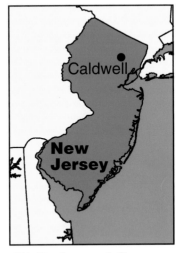

Birthplace of Grover Cleveland

Big Steve

Stephen Grover Cleveland was born in Caldwell, New Jersey, on March 18, 1837. As a child, he was big for his age. So people called him Big Steve.

Big Steve was the fifth of Richard and Ann Cleveland's nine children. His father was a Presbyterian minister.

When Big Steve was four, his family moved to Fayetteville, New York. He attended Fayetteville Academy. After school, he liked to swim, fish, and play in the woods.

When Big Steve was 13, his family moved to Clinton, New York. Then he visited his Uncle Lewis Allen in Buffalo, New York. Big Steve liked Buffalo and wanted to stay longer. But he had to go home.

Back in Clinton, Richard Cleveland's salary was not enough to support the family. In 1852, Big Steve worked in a general store to help out.

In 1853, Big Steve's father became ill. His father took an easier job in Holland Patent, New York. So the Clevelands moved there. But soon, Big Steve's father died.

Later that year, Big Steve became a teacher at the New York Institution for the Blind. But the school was run poorly. And the children were mistreated. Big Steve was upset that he could not change these things. So he quit.

In 1855, Big Steve decided to move to Cleveland, Ohio. He set off with a friend on the Erie Canal. On the way, he stopped in Buffalo to visit his Uncle Allen.

Grover Cleveland's birthplace in Caldwell, New Jersey

New York Lawyer

*C*leveland's uncle convinced him to stay in Buffalo. He helped Cleveland get a job as a clerk at a law office. Cleveland read law books. He learned from the lawyers.

Soon Cleveland became interested in politics. In 1856, he worked on **Democrat** James Buchanan's presidential campaign. Buchanan won the election.

In 1859, Cleveland passed the **bar exam**. Then he was **promoted** to chief clerk.

Three years later, Cleveland was elected supervisor of the city's second ward. In November of that year, he became assistant **district attorney**. He often won all of his cases each day.

In 1863, Cleveland was chosen to serve in the **Civil War**. But his brothers Lewis and Richard were already soldiers. So if Cleveland went to war, there would be no one to support his mother and sisters.

But the Conscription Act of 1863 said a man could hire someone to go in his place. So Cleveland hired a substitute.

In 1865, Cleveland ran for Erie County **district attorney**. He lost the election. So he continued to practice law. In 1870, he ran for sheriff of Erie County. This time, he won.

As sheriff, Cleveland worked well with lawyers. He kept the jail clean. And he served **warrants** promptly. He also **executed convicted** prisoners himself, instead of passing the responsibility to others.

In 1873, Cleveland's term as sheriff ended. For the next nine years, he practiced law in Buffalo.

President James Buchanan

The Veto Mayor

*I*n 1881, **Democrats nominated** Cleveland for mayor of Buffalo. Cleveland won the election. He **vetoed** many dishonest bills. He was known as the "Veto Mayor."

In 1882, the city council passed a bill for a new sewer system. Council members raised the price of the project. They wanted to keep the extra money. Cleveland vetoed their bill. He passed a bill to hire an engineer with a fair price.

Cleveland's honest **reputation** grew. The Democrats nominated him for governor of New York in 1882. He won the election in a landslide.

Governor Cleveland took office in 1883. He conducted business in public. His office was often crowded with people while he worked. This stopped anyone from asking for special favors or making secret deals.

As governor, Cleveland continued to veto dishonest bills. He also passed a law to inspect banks and **trusts** every year. He helped get a new **aqueduct** in New York. And he signed a bill to preserve the land around Niagara Falls.

In 1884, **Democrats nominated** Cleveland for president. The **Republicans** nominated James G. Blaine. Many Republicans distrusted Blaine. They voted for Cleveland instead.

It was a close election. Both candidates were accused of cheating. But after three days of recounting the votes, Cleveland won.

A poster from Grover Cleveland's 1884 campaign

The Making of the Twenty-second and Twenty-fourth United States President

1837
Born March 18 in Caldwell, New Jersey

1841
Family moves to Fayetteville, New York

1850
Family moves to Clinton, New York

1852
Works in a general store

1853
Family moves to Holland Patent, New York; father dies; teaches in New York City

1881
Elected mayor of Buffalo, New York

1882
Elected governor of New York

Historic Events during Cleveland's Presidencies

★ First modern Olympic games held in Athens

★ Henry Ford builds his first car

★ First professional football game played in Latrobe, Pennsylvania

★ Gustave Eiffel builds the Eiffel Tower in Paris

★ First U.S. Open Golf Championship

★ George Eastman perfects the Kodak box camera

1889
Moves to New York City; practices law

1892
Sherman Silver Purchase Act passes; elected president

Grover Cleveland

"Your every voter, as surely as your chief magistrate, exercises a public trust."

1855
Moves to Buffalo, New York; studies law

1859
Passes bar exam

1862
Elected supervisor of second ward; appointed assistant district attorney

1865
Runs for district attorney and loses

1870
Elected sheriff of Erie County

1884
Elected president

1885
Vice President Thomas Hendricks dies

1886
Signs Presidential Succession Act and Dawes Act; marries Frances Folsom

1887
Tenure of Office Act repealed

1888
Loses presidential election

PRESIDENTIAL YEARS

1893
Depression begins; Sherman Silver Purchase Act repealed

1894
Pullman strike

1897
Writes Great Britain and Venezuela treaty; moves to Princeton, New Jersey

1901
Becomes a trustee of Princeton University

1908
Dies on June 24

PRESIDENTIAL YEARS

President Cleveland

*C*leveland took office on March 4, 1885. His first task was to name his **cabinet** and fill many civil-service jobs. Usually, a new president fills these jobs with people from his own party. This is called the spoils system.

Cleveland was the first **Democratic** president in 24 years. So **Republicans** held many of the civil-service jobs. They did not want Cleveland to replace them with Democrats.

So Republicans reminded Cleveland about the Tenure of Office Act. It said that the president could not remove people from office without **Senate** approval.

But Cleveland felt that the president was not accountable to the Senate. This is called executive privilege. He also did not like the spoils system.

So he filled the positions with qualified people, whether they were Democrats or not. Then he worked to **repeal** the Tenure of Office Act. **Congress** repealed it two years later.

President Cleveland (front row, second from left) poses with his cabinet.

On November 25, 1885, Vice President Thomas Hendricks died. That December, Cleveland spoke to **Congress** about the Bland-Allison Act. It allowed the government to make money from silver as well as from gold.

Cleveland thought the Bland-Allison Act threatened the U.S. **economy**. He supported the **gold standard**. He felt that silver was worth less than gold. He wanted Congress to **repeal** the act.

Ever since Vice President Hendricks died, Cleveland had worried about who would be president if he died, too. So in January 1886, he signed the **Presidential Succession Act**.

In February of that year, he signed the Dawes Act. This act granted Native Americans citizenship and a land grant. But first they had to give up their reservation land.

In June 1886, Cleveland married Frances Folsom. He was the first president to be married in the White House.

Near the end of 1887, the U.S. Treasury had a large **surplus**. Cleveland thought the nation's high **tariffs** caused the surplus. He asked Congress to lower tariffs. He thought this would improve the economy. And the lower prices would help Americans.

In 1888, the **Democrats renominated** Cleveland. The **Republicans** nominated Benjamin Harrison. The election of 1888 was one of the most unusual in U.S. history.

The wedding of Grover Cleveland and Frances Folsom

An Early Retirement

*T*he election of 1888 was a close race. President Cleveland had 90,000 more popular votes than Harrison. But Harrison had 233 **electoral votes** to Cleveland's 168.

The U.S. **Constitution** says that the president is elected by the electoral college and not by the popular vote. So Harrison won the election.

In 1889, the Clevelands moved to New York City. Cleveland worked as a lawyer. In 1892, the Clevelands had their first child, Ruth. They went on to have four more children.

Cleveland spoke out against the Sherman Silver Purchase Act of 1892. It allowed both gold and silver to represent U.S. money. Cleveland still felt that silver was worth less than gold.

Some **Democrats** disagreed with Cleveland about the **gold standard**. But most remembered his honesty. The Democrats **nominated** him for president in 1892. The **Republicans** renominated President Benjamin Harrison.

During the campaign, a strike happened in Homestead, Pennsylvania. President Harrison sent troops there to stop it. This angered Americans. So Cleveland easily won the election.

Electoral Votes, 1888

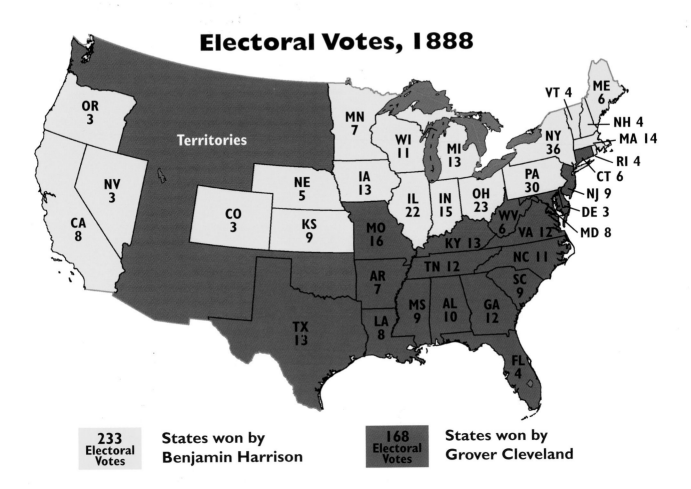

OR 3	Territories	MN 7				VT 4	ME 6
NV 3		WI 11	MI 13		NY 36		NH 4
	NE 5	IA 13		PA 30			MA 14
CA 8	CO 3	IL 22	IN 15	OH 23			RI 4
	KS 9	MO 16	KY 13	WV 6	VA 12		CT 6
		AR 7	TN 12	NC 11			NJ 9
TX 13	MS 9	AL 10	GA 12	SC 9			DE 3
	LA 8		FL 4				MD 8

| 233 Electoral Votes | States won by Benjamin Harrison | 168 Electoral Votes | States won by Grover Cleveland |

Each state has electoral votes equal to the number of representatives it has in Congress. The state's population determines its number of representatives. States with large populations get more electoral votes.

When a candidate wins a state's popular vote, he or she wins its electoral votes. Grover Cleveland won more popular votes than Benjamin Harrison. But the states that Harrison won had more electoral votes. So Harrison won the 1888 election.

President Once More

*C*leveland took office on March 4, 1893. Earlier that year, Americans had seized control of Hawaii. They asked the U.S. to **annex** it. But Cleveland felt they had taken control of Hawaii unfairly. So he stopped **Congress** from annexing it.

In May 1893, a **depression** began. Cleveland blamed it on the Sherman Silver Purchase Act. So he worked with Congress and **repealed** the act.

As time went on, the depression worsened. Americans began to **riot** and strike. The worst strike happened in Chicago, Illinois, at the Pullman Palace Car Company. Its workers made railroad cars. They felt their wages had been cut unfairly. So in 1894, they went on strike.

The Pullman strike blocked railroad traffic. This meant the U.S. mail could not be delivered. So Cleveland sent troops to Chicago. They stopped the strike.

By 1895, U.S. gold supplies had become very low. This worsened the depression. So Cleveland asked bankers to buy government **bonds**. The bankers paid for the bonds in gold. This renewed U.S. gold supplies.

In 1896, Cleveland made Utah a state. The next year, he arranged a treaty between Great Britain and Venezuela. It worked to solve a border disagreement between Venezuela and Great Britain's colony, British Guiana.

Cleveland did not want to run for president again. He and his family left the White House in March 1897.

The United States during Cleveland's presidency

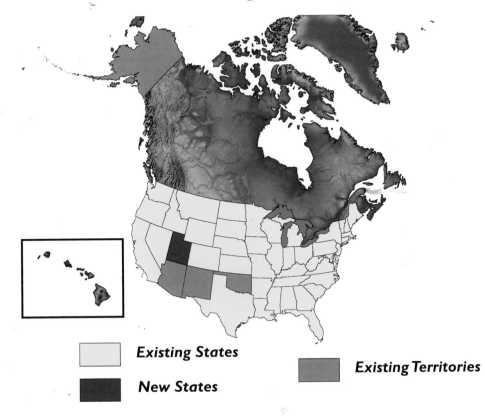

Existing States

New States

Existing Territories

The Seven "Hats" of the U.S. President

To be president, a person must have lived in the country for at least 14 years, must be a U.S. citizen born in America, and must be at least 35 years old.

A president is elected or re-elected every four years.

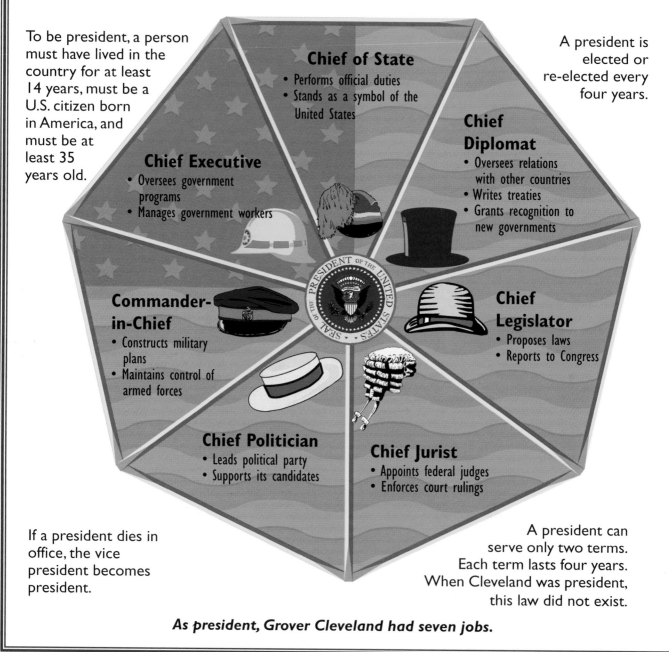

Chief of State
- Performs official duties
- Stands as a symbol of the United States

Chief Executive
- Oversees government programs
- Manages government workers

Chief Diplomat
- Oversees relations with other countries
- Writes treaties
- Grants recognition to new governments

Commander-in-Chief
- Constructs military plans
- Maintains control of armed forces

Chief Legislator
- Proposes laws
- Reports to Congress

Chief Politician
- Leads political party
- Supports its candidates

Chief Jurist
- Appoints federal judges
- Enforces court rulings

If a president dies in office, the vice president becomes president.

A president can serve only two terms. Each term lasts four years. When Cleveland was president, this law did not exist.

As president, Grover Cleveland had seven jobs.

The Three Branches of the U.S. Government

Congress is in the Capitol Building in Washington, D.C. It can pass laws and stop the president's veto. Congress can also change the Constitution to stop the president's plans or Supreme Court rulings.

The president lives in the White House in Washington, D.C. He or she can stop (veto) laws passed by Congress, and propose new laws. The president can also choose Supreme Court judges.

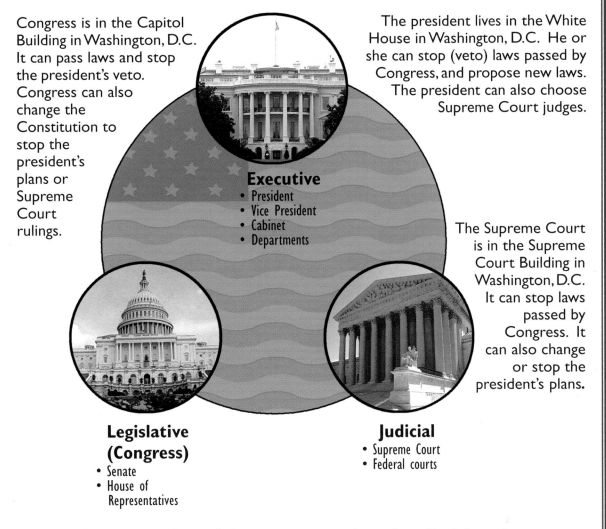

Executive
- President
- Vice President
- Cabinet
- Departments

The Supreme Court is in the Supreme Court Building in Washington, D.C. It can stop laws passed by Congress. It can also change or stop the president's plans.

Legislative (Congress)
- Senate
- House of Representatives

Judicial
- Supreme Court
- Federal courts

The U.S. Constitution formed three government branches. Each branch has power over the others. So no single group or person can control the country. The Constitution calls this "separation of powers."

Cleveland Retires

*T*he Cleveland family moved to Princeton, New Jersey. They settled in a home they called Westland.

Cleveland always found time to hunt and fish. He wrote articles and gave speeches. And he became active at Princeton University. In 1901, Cleveland became a Princeton **trustee**.

In 1904, Cleveland's daughter Ruth died suddenly. This saddened the entire Cleveland family.

After Ruth's death, Cleveland continued to give speeches and write. But his health grew poor. He suffered from several heart attacks. He died on June 24, 1908.

Grover Cleveland brought honesty and honor to all of his public offices. As president, he fought for the **gold standard**. And he led the country through a **depression**. Some of his beliefs made him unpopular. But no matter what, he always stood up for what he thought was right.

Opposite page: Fishing was one of Cleveland's favorite ways to relax.

Fast Facts

- Cleveland was the first president to use fireworks at his **inauguration**.

- The Clevelands' daughter Esther was the first child born in the White House.

- Many people think the candy bar "Baby Ruth" was named after the famous baseball player, Babe Ruth. In fact, it was named after President Cleveland's daughter Ruth.

- During Cleveland's second presidency, he discovered cancer in his mouth. He needed surgery. But he did not want to worry Americans. So he kept his illness and surgery a secret.

- Cleveland advised the U.S. to accept the Statue of Liberty from France. He dedicated the statue in October 1886.

The Statue of Liberty was a gift from France. It honored the United States' one hundredth birthday.

Glossary

annex - to add land to a nation.

aqueduct - a pipe that carries water over long distances.

bar exam - the test a person must pass to become a lawyer.

bond - a certificate sold by a government that promises to pay its purchase price plus interest at a given future date.

cabinet - a group of advisers chosen by the president.

Civil War - a war between groups in the same country. The United States of America and the Confederate States of America fought a civil war from 1861 to 1865.

Congress - the lawmaking body of the U.S. It is made up of the Senate and the House of Representatives.

Constitution - the document that states the supreme law in the United States. Each state has a constitution, too.

convict - to prove someone guilty of a crime.

Democrat - one of the two main political parties in the United States. Democrats are often liberal and believe in large government.

depression - a period of time when there is little buying and selling, and many people are out of work.

district attorney - a lawyer for the government that works in a specific district, such as a county or state.

economy - the way a country uses its money, goods, and natural resources.

electoral votes - votes cast by the electoral college. The electoral college is a group that elects the president and vice president. After a presidential election, each state sends its representatives to the electoral college. There, they vote for their party's candidate.

execute - to put to death in accordance with the law.

gold standard - a system in which the dollar is defined as a fixed amount of gold, there is unlimited coinage of gold, currency is fully redeemable in gold, and gold can be freely imported and exported.

inaugurate - to be sworn into office.

nominate - to name a candidate for office.

Presidential Succession Act - a law that says who will fill the office of president in case the president and vice president both die. The order of succession is: president, vice president, Speaker of the House of Representatives, pro tempore of the Senate, then the members of the president's cabinet in the order that their departments were created.

promote - to advance in rank or position.

repeal - to formally withdraw or cancel.

Republican - one of the two main political parties in the United States. Republicans are often conservative and believe in small government.

reputation - what people think about someone.

riot - a disorderly, often violent disturbance by a large crowd.

Senate - a group of 100 elected senators, two from each state, that makes laws for the country.

surplus - an amount over what is needed.

tariff - fees or taxes on shipped goods.

trust - a business that illegally controls a certain good or service, which stops competition.

trustee - someone who supervises business matters.

veto - the right of one member of a decision-making group to stop an action by the group. In the U.S. government, the president can veto bills passed by Congress. But Congress can override the president's veto with a two-thirds majority vote.

warrant - a document that authorizes something, such as an arrest.

Internet Sites

The Presidents of the United States of America
http://www.whitehouse.gov/WH/glimpse/presidents/html/presidents.html
This site is part of the White House Web site.
American Presidents Series
http://www.americanpresidents.org
This site from PBS has information on every president.
Interlink cafe: U.S. presidents
http://www.interlink-cafe.com/uspresidents/22nd.htm
This site has links to Cleveland's home, his inaugural address, and more.

These sites are subject to change. Go to your favorite search engine and type in "United States Presidents" for more sites.

Index

jB
CLEVELAN
D

Joseph, Paul.

Grover Cleveland.

$21.35

DATE			